MW00397319

HUMOR
THROUGH HELL

A Cartoon Record of an American POW's
Experience in WWII Prison Camps

Rob,
I remember our
trip. Wish for more!
Semper Fi,
Bob Ehrhart

HUMOR
THROUGH HELL

A Cartoon Record of an American POW's Experience in WWII Prison Camps

"SWEET DREAMS"

ROBERT EHRHART

As described to
Jan Thompson

Foreword by Loretta Swit

Copyright © 2015 by Robert Ehrhart

All rights reserved. No portion of this book may be reproduced—mechanically, electronically, or by any other means, including photocopying—without written permission of the copyright holder.

ISBN-13: 978-1499359923
ISBN-10: 1499359926

Cover design services provided by George T. Dotson
Interior design and production services by Susan Malikowski, DesignLeaf Studio
Editorial services provided by Susan H. Wilson

Text set in Adobe Simoncini Garamond and Brandon, Hannes von Doehren.
Display type set in ITC/Bitstream Bailey Sans.

Printed by CreateSpace, an Amazon.com company.
Manufactured in the United States of America.
Available from Amazon.com, CreateSpace.com, and other retail outlets.

10 9 8 7 6 5 4 3 2 1

Dedication

To my dear friend and fellow Fourth Marine

Martin "Ike" Eichmann

who watched my back at Camp Cabanatuan

With Thanks

This book would never have been completed without the energy and help of my friend Dolores Frank. She encouraged me to see the project through to completion and has been diligent in ensuring that I receive recognition for my work. This is my story, but without Dolores's assistance, it would not be available for others.

Also, I want to thank my friend documentary filmmaker Jan Thompson, for recognizing the value of my cartoons—and of my experiences during the war—to posterity. It was through Jan's thorough interviews and her careful work on their transcriptions that this book took form.

Contents

CONTENTS

CONTENTS

CONTENTS

CONTENTS

Foreword

LORETTA SWIT

Former P.O.W., Private First Class Bob Ehrhart, has given us a collection of memories
in the form of cartoons—simultaneously painful and humorously black. They invoke tears
as well as winces, smiles and heartaches. He presents us with an insightful look at life as he
lived it in the Japanese P.O.W. camps during World War II.

We have this collection because of his courage and determination despite the ever-present
threat of punishment and death.

After being discovered a first time, Bob was punished severely, and his drawings were
destroyed. He re-created the present set from memory, moving them hidden, from camp
to camp during the remainder of his imprisonment.

The book is a tribute to his courage and resilience, his faith, his wit, and his survival.

It was my privilege to have met him and thanked him.

Introduction

I am a documentary filmmaker and a college professor. I am also the daughter of a World War II Pacific theater POW. My dad's war experiences—those he shared with his children and those he did not—fueled my interest in exploring through television documentaries the POW experience under imperial Japan.

I first met former Fourth Marine and Japanese POW camp survivor Robert Ehrhart in 1994 at an American Defenders of Bataan & Corregidor (ADBC) reunion (the Fourth Marines had their reunions at the same time the ADBC had theirs). We were introduced by Richard Long, head of the Oral History unit at the Marine Corps History and Museums Division. Dick had interviewed over the years several marines and Bob was next on his list of likely interviewees, not only because of his ability to contribute to the growing oral history of the war in Asia but because Bob had a collection of his own cartoons drawn at the time of his POW experience. Dick was interested in obtaining Bob's cartoons for the museum, which he was eventually able to do.

On the afternoon of June 2, 1994, Dick and I met with Bob. Also in attendance were another former Fourth Marine and camp mate, Wilbur Marrs, and Jeff Russell, the nephew of a Fourth Marine doing research on his uncle's service. This was the first time I had seen Bob's cartoons, and it took me only seconds to realize how unique and special they were, and how worthy of preservation and dissemination. The cartoons were Bob's own pictorial diary of his POW experience under the Imperial Japanese Army. Early in the research stage of my documentary project I found that few contemporary "visuals" had survived over time (or had existed in the first place). Bob's 115 cartoons are a historic testament to the events of a certain time and place. Their humor and pathos reflect the strength of a young soldier determined to survive a brutal, and long, captivity.

This session with Bob and Wilbur Marrs lasted about two hours. Though Bob and I stayed in touch through the years, I did not see Bob again until April 2012 when we were traveling together to the Philippine Islands for the 70th Memorial Ghost Soldier's Valor Tour. We discussed in more detail the idea of creating a book of his cartoons, and I later visited him at his home several times to obtain more background information, to flesh out captions for the cartoons, and to add historical context. Bob was very forthcoming during our conversations. I found his memory of the events surrounding his war experiences to be clear, detailed, and consistent. This book is the product of our work together. Bob's voice tells his own story in his own words in the introductions to each of the parts as well as in the cartoon captions themselves.

This book of Bob's cartoons is divided into five parts, beginning with part 1: Bob's enlistment in the Marines in September 1940 at the age of seventeen, his assignment to an anti-aircraft unit at the Cavite Naval Yard in the Philippines; his unit's transfer to Bataan, then Corregidor and Fort Hughes; and the surrender of the American and Filipino forces and his initial incarceration at the 92d Garage at Corregidor. The cartoons in part 2 depict Bob's experiences from June 1942 through mid-September 1943 at Camp Cabanatuan on Luzon, where he met survivors of the Bataan Death March, learned to cope with POW camp life, viewed the infamous camp hospital Zero Ward, and served on horrific burial details. In this camp Bob began to draw his cartoons in earnest, in order to record what went on around him (and against him) but also to boost his own morale and that of his fellow POWs.

In part 3, from October 1943 to May 1945, Bob's story continues from his transfer by hell ship to Camp Sakurajima, near Osaka, to perform slave labor in the Osaka Ship Yards while living in a POW camp within a large Japanese urban area. His cartoons reflect POW life in this setting—working closely with Japanese civilians and surviving their attempts to injure or kill him, living under constant hostile surveillance, and even contributing to the Allied war effort through sabotage. The American bombing of Osaka forced the relocation of the prisoners to Akenobe, a camp in the mountainous region in northwest Japan. Part 4 contains Bob's cartoons depicting the life of a POW in the Akenobe Mitsubishi copper mine. Weighing at most one hundred pounds, Bob and his compatriots endured starvation rations and the abuse of a mining "honcho" named The Madman. In part 5, the Japanese surrender in August 1945 liberates the POWs; Bob eventually makes his way home to California and ends up at the front door of his parent's house.

Bob, through his cartoons, gave witness to the atrocities committed against the POWs— and the rare act of grace by an incarcerator. He testified to the importance of food in the lives and mindsets of men so long starved that he drew them as living skeletons dressed in rags. Dysentery, vermin, long hours of forced labor, squalid living conditions—all became grist for Bob's gentle humor and artistic talent. With great wisdom for one so young, Bob understood the importance of humor to the survival of his fellow POWs. The cartoons are at once a snapshot of individual events and a record of how the POWs lived and often died.

At incredible personal risk, Bob drew his cartoons throughout his entire imprisonment, using as his media the backs of Carnation condensed milk can labels, envelopes, whatever scrap of paper was available. On the fronts he wrote between lines of type a diary of atrocities and events. He secreted the cartoons in sheets of toilet paper. It was in Camp Sakurajima one winter's day that his cache of cartoons was discovered during a "strafing" (a detailed search) of his barracks. Forced to wait over a week for his incarcerators to level punishment, Bob expected to be executed. He was instead tied up, suspended from a flag pole with his feet just barely touching the ground, and beaten severely until unconscious. His fellow POWs cut him down and moved him to their barracks to help him recover, warming him near a fire made from their own meager stash of coal. Bob thought the Japanese were so angry over the cartoons that they neglected to turn them over to find his diary entries—if they had, he would have most certainly been executed. As soon as he recovered sufficiently from his injuries, Bob recreated the cartoons from memory, often with the help of his fellow POWs.

All during his imprisonment Bob intentionally worked to survive but, as he is still proud to relate, never at the cost of another man's life. Since he intended to chronicle what went on around him, he incorporated into each cartoon a location identifier stamp, a kind of chop. The stamp for Cabanatuan was a quan can, for Sakurajima, a teapot, for Akenobe, a spoon. He claims to this very day that drawing the cartoons kept him sane.

It is interesting to note that Bob did not pursue a career in the arts after liberation. Upon his return to the states, he lived a normal life. Bob applied to UC Berkeley and was admitted in June 1946; he graduated with a bachelor's degree in mechanical engineering four years later. He married Winifred, the love of his life, following a doctor's warning that he would most likely not live to see their fiftieth wedding anniversary given the state of his health at the time of his repatriation. Winifred's death, he said to me once, was worse than any of his experiences as a POW. I believe him.

In the Philippines, 1941

This photo was taken shortly after I arrived in the Philippines.

A family photo following my return from the war.

This photo was taken after I returned home from Japan and rehab. I'm wearing my uniform. My dad, William, is standing next to me. My mother, Ethel, is the woman in the center who is looking in my direction. The rest of the folks are friends of the family.

Vietnam, 2013

Here I am back in Asia, this time in Vietnam in 2013.

American Defenders Memorial Reunion, 2014

Celebrating with two good friends, documentary filmmaker Jan Thompson (center) and Dolores Frank (left), at the May 2014 meeting of the American Defenders of Bataan and Corregidor Memorial Society in San Jose, California.

HUMOR
THROUGH HELL

A Cartoon Record of an American POW's
Experience in WWII Prison Camps

ENLISTMENT AND WAR

SEPTEMBER 1940 – MAY 1942

I was born June 4, 1923 in Oakland, California. I attended Fremont High School there and took as many art and math classes that I could. I loved drawing old sailing ships—square riggers—and horses, stuff that boys were interested in. During the Depression Dad lost his job and had to go on relief as many people did back in those days. Dad ended up driving a truck for Mayflower Creamery, and I worked for them, too, for awhile. I had a job repainting the letters on the truck and also worked as a maintenance man.

A kid in my neighborhood had joined the Marines and would come home and walk down the street in his uniform. I'd talk to him about what it was like. So, when I was seventeen, I enlisted in the United States Marine Corps Reserves in September of 1940. Within less than two months I was on active duty and sent to San Diego. In April of 1941, when I was in the Marines for only about seven months, I was on the USS Henderson bound for the Philippine Islands. My dad, who had been a Marine in World War I, sailed on that same ship to France in 1917!

The first officer that I had was Gunner Beale, and he was a real "so and so." He had us march twenty miles with packs and ammunition in the hot tropical sun. These marches were really hard but he probably saved our lives later on because we were so tough and disciplined.

I was stationed at the Cavite Naval Yard and I remember one day in December the bugle sounded a call we weren't familiar with. We hadn't heard it before and an old timer said "That's the call to arms!" We didn't know what to do. What was the uniform of the day? We were told "rifles and bayonets!" since the Japs had bombed Pearl Harbor and war had started.

We were issued live ammunition. I was assigned to a machine gun unit, which was exactly what my dad had told me to avoid since these units were always attacked by the enemy. Our unit had an old World War I water-cooled machine gun on a cart with wagon wheels. I attached to the machine gun cart a book of the complete works of Shakespeare, which I had found in a building in Cavite that I had been guarding, and dragged it around. On guard there were usually two of us and I would read Shakespeare out loud. I really liked Shakespeare, especially Julius Caesar's quote: "Cowards die many times before their deaths; the valiant never taste of death but once." I must have been a coward since I'm still here!

My unit was later transferred for a few weeks to Bataan and then to the island of Corregidor. I was only on Corregidor for a couple of days before we were transferred to Fort Hughes on Caballo Island. I again manned a machine gun position. The Japs shelled us, and I caught some shrapnel in the arm so I was sent to the hospital in Malinta Tunnel back on Corregidor. This was on April 8, just about when the troops were folding up on Bataan, right before the surrender. The hospital corridors were getting filled up with wounded so I left without orders and went back to my unit on Fort Hughes. The situation was chaotic and it was impossible to obtain orders.

Bataan surrendered on April 9, and then the Japs began to shell Corregidor Island and Fort Hughes every day. They shelled us on the beach, and a bomb hit just in front of my machine gun and knocked me out. I came to and had blood coming out of my nose and ears. I was dazed—we were all dazed so we retreated to the tunnel. There were a whole bunch of people in there—Marines and Army guys both. They said we had surrendered. Some of the guys were crying, literally. We didn't want to surrender: we were surrendered. This event was probably the most emotional time in my life. Everyone was crying—not because we were scared but because we had failed. I can remember one of the army officers still had his sidearm. And I, a lousy private, said to him, "Sir, you better get rid of that." He handed it to me and I field stripped it and threw the pieces out. We had a white flag flying but the Japs kept firing at us until they landed.

We heard gibberish outside the tunnel and someone told us to come out. We all had the same thought–the Japs had killed a crew over on Bataan, that they had not allowed them to surrender. We figured when we walked out that that was the end. As I walked out of the tunnel I was scared out of my mind. My arms and hands were straight up in the air, and a Jap next to me pulled my arms down and laughed as though to say, "You stupid ass!" It was a nice laugh. And I thought, "Well, maybe I am going to live."

They marched us out, lined us up along the road, and counted us off (bango, in Japanese)— the first time I heard "ichi ni . . ." They gave us cans of food, which happened to be ketchup and a lot of other junk we globbered down because we had hardly eaten in so long. They bedded us down in one of the barracks that still was partially standing. And they didn't beat us.

In the morning the Japs kicked me in the ribs and woke me up. There were about fifteen of us and they took us out to the shore where the barbwire, guns, and land mines had been. Our captors pointed that we were going out to the barges, so we had to walk through our barbwire and land mine field. After we got to the barges a Jap poked me with a bayonet. Next to him on the barge was a water can. He gestured that I should drink some water. We had not had anything to drink for over a day and were terribly thirsty, so I unscrewed it, took a drink, and reached for my canteen. His bayonet came down and I understood the word nie. He was nice to a point.

They took us over to Corregidor to the 92d Garage (the site of a motor pool for the 92d Coast Artillery, hence the name), where we joined the prisoners from Corregidor. I went out on my own and built a shelter half. I joined the burial detail because I didn't have anything with me, not even food. So I separated myself from the detail and entered the Malinta Tunnel where I picked up some food rations—WWI elk—and I put them in a gas mask bag. As I was walking out of the tunnel there was a Jap with his rifle. He signaled me to "come here" and he patted me down. I motioned "food." He didn't do anything, just laughed and pushed me away. He was a soldier—and they weren't all soldiers. These were the guys who fought us.

We cleaned up the battlefield, and the bodies were burned. We picked up the dog tags and put them in a big pile in Malinta Tunnel. I didn't have my dog tags–I can't remember if I had thrown them away. But I knew I didn't want to die because I understood that my body would not have been identified.

PART 1. ENLISTMENT AND WAR CARTOONS

Cartoon 1. "Up to Date Equipment"

We arrived at the Cavite Naval Base in the Philippines on December 9, 1941, and were given a short course in the operation of a 3-inch antiaircraft gun. Up until then, most, probably all, of A Company was experienced in weapons no larger than .50-caliber machine guns or 37 mm antitank guns. I was assigned to E Battery on top of the Naval Ammunition Depot. The next day we were attacked. I remember an officer trying to shoot at the airplanes with his .45! All of our weapons were from World War I and could do nothing to repel the modern Japanese weapons.

Cartoon 2 (sketch). "Corregidor"

This drawing represents my time on Corregidor and Fort Hughes. My machine gun position on Fort Hughes was painstakingly dug in gravel and rock. A sheet metal frame was first built and gradually forced into the gravel bed as we dug around it. The pit was then covered with timbers and "sandbags" of soil. The bottom corner represents the 92d Garage where the Japs herded us POWS.

Cartoon 3. "Sentry on Duty (?) or Once in a Lifetime"

It was not unusual for a sentry to be tempted when guarding a food supply. Our rations had been cut several times and a lot of our canned food was from World War I.

Cartoon 4. "What's Dis an' Where's Da Rest or An Introduction to Rice"

Supplies such as food and medicine were not getting through to the Philippines. We had our last decent meal in a bivouac on Bataan on Christmas Day in '41. On our march to this first bivouac in the field, we had only the field rations we carried in our packs (for many it was only GI issue—Ration "D"—chocolate bars) and only the water in our canteens. I was on Bataan for about three weeks and then ordered to transfer to Corregidor Island. We had heard that the soldiers on Corregidor were eating better than we were, so on arrival we expected a full meal. Instead we were introduced to skimpy rations of rice and canned abalone, which were gradually decreased to starvation levels.

Cartoon 5. "No Time for Rank"

I was only on Corregidor long enough for the first bombing. They seemed to order me to wherever the next bombing would take place. When I wasn't in a foxhole I was manning a machine gun on the beach. We were getting shelled every day, and one shell hit right in front of our gun. These were water-cooled machine guns, and the water jacket was damaged and the water was running out. I was bleeding from mouth and nose. We were all dazed so we took off for the next line of defense, behind the battery fortress.

Cartoon 6. "Sittin' It Out! Sweatin' It Out"

There was more than a little contempt, and some envy, for the Malinta "tunnel rats." After Bataan surrendered, the Imperial Japanese shelled Corregidor daily. Malinta Tunnel housed the hospital and headquarters in comparative safety. General Douglas MacArthur got the nickname "Dug-Out Doug" because he never came out of the tunnel—that is, not until he escaped to Australia.

Cartoon 7. "Barbwire Detail"

Eventually I was assigned to Fort Hughes on Caballo, a smaller island not far from Corregidor, also known as Fort Mills. Fort Hughes, Fort Drum, and Fort Frank were fortified islands. I was ordered to help place barbwire down on the beaches. You felt like a fish in a barrel on these barbwire details because the beach was open and cliffs were at your back. The Japs had their 105 mm howitzers set up on the beaches of Bataan and sighted in on our beach.

Cartoon 8. "The P-40 Flys Again or Air Superiority"

About eight hours after they bombed Pearl, nearly sinking our entire naval fleet, the Japs bombed Clark Air Field on Luzon. The Japs caught our planes on the ground and destroyed our "air force." After the Clark Field fiasco, we had several P40s, but we saw them so infrequently we referred to our air force as "the P40." Our planes were no match for the fast Jap Zero.

Cartoon 9. "Corregidor Still Stands (Although Slightly Shaky)"

Radio broadcasts from the States repeatedly ended with "Corregidor still stands." Of course, we knew it would be still standing after the Japs swept over us. Most of us had no concept of surrender, though we knew it would be impossible for reinforcements to reach us in time.

Cartoon 10. "Water Line"

After the surrender on Corregidor, the 12,000 survivors were herded into a two-block area called the 92d Garage, formerly a repair facility for the 92d Coast Artillery. I was taken there from Fort Hughes. This was an open space in the hot sun and it looked like a veritable hobo jungle. Shelters were created from any material that was available. The stench was awful because there were no latrines and from the rotting bodies. Clouds of flies would land and stick to your face. We had to scrounge for food and spend hours in the hot sun in the long water line. Men would take turns standing in line with several of their buddies' canteens because the Japs would sometimes turn off the water. We were held there several weeks awaiting assignment to our POW camp.

CAMP CABANATUAN, PHILIPPINES

JUNE 1, 1942 - SEPTEMBER 17, 1943

The Japs moved us from the 92d Garage and then marched us down the main boulevard to Camp Cabanatuan, northeast of Corregidor on Luzon. We were the first people sent to that camp. We Marines and some Navy sailors were assigned to one of the barracks.

Eventually POWs came in from Camp O'Donnell—the camp where all of the Bataan survivors had first gone to just off the Death March. They were in really bad shape and started dying like flies. I was on the burial detail again. The Japs put Marines and Navy on that detail because they were in better physical condition. We went to the hospital area—because that's where the sick and injured were sent to die—and four of us carried the litters. You would put the dead on the stretchers and their skin would stick to your hands since they had been dead for several days. We wrapped wet rags around our faces because of the stench. We just threw their bodies in the pit. I worked three solid months without a day off.

There was one POW I'll never forget. He had been shot and killed by a Jap soldier who had enticed him too close to the barbwire fence with food or something, just for the fun of it. Well, his body was swollen up something terrible, and when we threw him into the pit his intestines came out of his anus. I almost vomited. I hated the burial detail; it was the worst detail I was ever on—though picking up the bodies on Corregidor and cleaning up the battlefield were also bad.

It was in Cabanatuan I started to draw. Unlike the POW camps in Japan, in the Philippine camps we were not constantly under the surveillance of the Japanese. The guards would enter the camp only on occasion for a "strafing run" (inspection). On these runs they would generally try to find some excuse to knock someone around; however, these raids were relatively infrequent, and if you were careful you could get away with fracturing a few rules. Most of us took advantage of this comparative freedom to engage in a number of hobbies.

One of my first efforts, and probably the most dangerous, was counterfeiting a twenty-dollar Japanese Occupation bill. I split the take with a soldier who pawned it off on a Jap who was doing an illicit business selling cigarettes through the fence after dusk. Cigarettes were like gold and helped get my friend "Ike" Eichmann and me into the rice flour business.

To bolster everybody's morale—my own and that of my over one hundred barracks mates —I started drawing my cartoons. I had a pencil, but since paper was impossible to obtain I bartered for whatever anyone had available. Around Christmas of '42 shipments of Carnation condensed milk arrived along with limes and onions. (Our death rate then dropped dramatically. In the preceding six-month period over twenty-five hundred POWs had perished. Consequently, most of the canned milk was issued to the hospital area.) What a bonanza for me! It seemed like everyone rounded up labels to give me for my cartoons. I used the label backs, which were almost white, for my cartoons and the label fronts, which were red and crowded with printed lettering, to record a diary of events and atrocities.

I made one drawing of a kid being executed. The Japs would make you kneel with your head sticking out, and this drawing showed the Jap standing over him with his sword. Another atrocity I drew pertained to the torture and execution of three officers who had failed in an attempt to escape. The Japs tied them up from the guard house so their feet just barely touched the ground. Native girls were forced to hit them with 2x4s when they walked by. I remember the girls crying and crying because they didn't want to do it. After several days, the Japs had the three officers dig their own graves and stood them up in front of a firing squad. U.S. execution squads were different in that a target was placed over the heart and everyone fired at once. But the Japanese at Cabanatuan fired at will, crack crack crack crack. The officers were moaning, and two of them were in agony. The Jap officer finally shot them in the head.

PART 2. CAMP CABANATUAN, PHILIPPINES, CARTOONS

Cartoon 11 (sketch). "Cabanatuan Barracks and Guard Towers"

I made this drawing while inside my barracks, looking out the window.

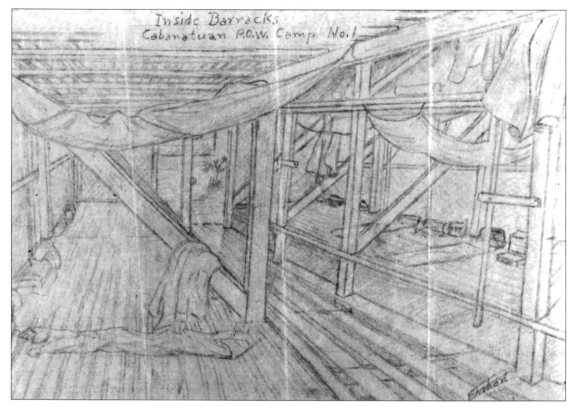

Cartoon 12. "Inside Barracks Cabanatuan P.O.W. Camp #1"

The Marines didn't want to get mixed up with the Army men. We didn't like the Army and didn't get along with them. We got along fine with Navy—that is, when we weren't drunk and fighting each other. Of course that was before the war. The barracks had two story bays. The Japs crammed as many POWs in there as they could. So we just laid next to each other, sometimes actually touching each other. Some of us had mosquito nets and others didn't.

Cartoon 13. "Ye Olde Well or Bucket, Bucket, Who'ze Gotta Nother Bucket"

It was several weeks at Camp No. 3 before the water system was operable. We depended on a single well for water. There was always some klutz who would lose the bucket down the shaft.

Cartoon 14. "Cabanatuan 'Turkey' Dinner"

My nineteenth birthday—June 4th, 1942—occurred shortly after we arrived in Cabanatuan. My buddy and fellow 4th Marine, Marty ("Ike") Eichmann, sold his class ring for food. He helped me celebrate by giving me a couple of his sardines.

Cartoon 15. "Laundry Day B.D."

The early days in Cabanatuan were as hard on the officers as on the enlisted men. Eventually the officers aquired "dog robbers"—enlisted men who would do work for the officer such as washing their clothing. As a result, the enlisted man would either get some extra food or even a cash payment.

Cartoon 16. "Delousing"

Lice became a problem after a while. However, I don't recall either the Navy or Marine barracks having anyone infected.

Cartoon 17. "A Restful (?) Nite"

Bedbugs were a constant problem. They would nest in between the bamboo slats we slept on and in the crevices in the nipa walls of the barracks. We would take the bamboo slats out of the bag and run them through a fire. Then we replaced the slats, but the vermin would eventually return.

Cartoon 18. "Saturday Nite or A Rare Sight"

Bathing was always a problem because there were no facilities. Most of us had to stand under the eaves in a rainshower and use the runoff. Since I was with the first group that entered the camp, I searched the area for anything of use and found a section of sheet metal duct that I pounded into a rectangular tub and kept filled with water. I shared it with a disabled friend who kept watch over it while I was at work. Many of the Army and National Guard personnel had limited field training and made little effort to keep clean, contributing to their higher death rate.

Cartoon 19. "Sweet Dreams"

Food was a constant obsession.

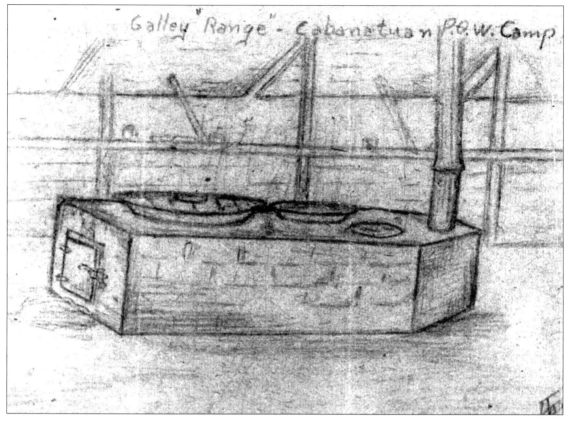

Cartoon 20. "Galley 'Range' —Cabanatuan P.O.W. Camp"

The kitchen was located in a separate building and in it were the kawalies or big pots. Wood from outside the camp was used for fuel. The usual meal was lugao, a Filipino word for a rice gruel. Sometimes there were some vegetable tops in the rice.

Cartoon 21. "Lougao vs. Rice Soup"

Sometimes there were two lines for chow because there was more than one kawali of rice in use. Not all "chefs" made the rice the same or with the proper ration of water to rice. It was a dreaded occurrence when a prisoner would find himself in the watery rice line.

Cartoon 22. "Barracks 13 — Burnt Rice!!"

There would always be a nice crust at the bottom of the kawali that would cook the rice. This was a "treat" but there wasn't enough to go around the camp. So it was scraped off and placed in five-gallon cans to be distributed to each barracks in turn.

Cartoon 23. "Scoffin'"

"Scoffin'" was the term for eating. If you wanted to live, you had to eat that rice and sometimes you had to swallow it twice (often it would make me gag and food would come back up). I would have to force myself to eat because there was no other food. You did things you thought you would never do.

Cartoon 24. "Vel Ze Da Mess Offizza! or Through the Galley"

In the futile hope that they could get a few extra grains of rice, some prisoners pounded out their mess gear to make it larger and then would thrust it quickly under the scoop. There were constant complaints that their rations were short.

Cartoon 25. "Quan Kitchen or There's Always Room for One More"

A stove was available for those lucky enough to have extra "food," which was very difficult to obtain. Albeit, the stove was usually very crowded. There was only one stove for about three thousand POWs.

Cartoon 26. "Home Cookin' (a la 'Quan')"

Quan was a term that meant anything extra to eat. This food could be anything from watercress to snakes and even rats and dog (I never ate dog). There were quan fires going on all over the compound. Sometimes, one of the officers would even ask permission to use an enlisted man's fire for his quan. You can tell this is an officer in the cartoon because of his "shiny" shoulder bars.

Cartoon 27. "A 'Doggone' Mystery"

A dog that belonged to one of the cooks mysteriously disappeared one night. It was rumored that he became a protein supplement to a GI's rice ration.

Cartoon 28. "Camp Butcher or Try, Try Again!"

A POW was assigned to butchering carabao, a kind of docile water buffalo, for the Japs. If we were lucky, the prisoners would get the hoofs and head for their soup. Sometimes we got nothing. But when we stood in line for chow, we always prayed that we'd get a small piece of meat or fat.

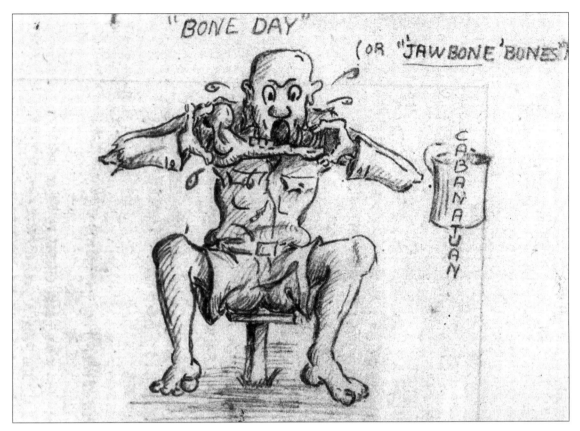

Cartoon 29. "Bone Day or 'Jawbone' Bones"

If by chance there were any bones given to the mess, lots were drawn to determine who would get the bones or bone.

Cartoon 30. "Chow Up or A Common Occurance"

When it rained, things became very sloppy and tragic. This cartoon's title is a twist on words because the British used the phrase "chow down" for sit down to eat.

Cartoon 31. "The Trots"

Along with hunger pangs, dysentery was always with us, though there were periods of remission. On every trip to the head there was fear of the return of blood and mucous because this could mean a death sentence.

Cartoon 32. Even the officers had problems . . .

Even the officers had problems with dysentery. The Naval officer pictured here asked me for a copy of this cartoon.

Cartoon 33. "Damn That Rice Coffee!!"

Most prisoners, probably because of a diet consisting of rice and watery soup, had to urinate ten to twenty times a night, especially in the cold weather. Rice coffee was made by charring raw rice then boiling it. One night when I was in the latrine a Brit came running in holding himself. Well, he didn't make it and he squirted me in the back of the legs. So I clobbered him and in his British whine he cried "Why did you have to do that?!" A good night's sleep was impossible: sometimes you would get back up in your bay and you would have to go again. So after nights like that you'd just fall asleep when taking a break while on a work detail.

Cartoon 34. "How Not to 'Make It'"

Trading food for just about anything was common in camp. Trading cigarettes for food was basically a death sentence for someone—I never traded my cigarettes for another person's food. This cartoon was inspired by the death of a friend who had been suffering from pellagra, one of the many diseases of malnutrition we suffered from. Symptoms of pellagra included loss of appetite and dementia, which led some of its victims to virtually starve themselves to death. No amount of reasoning could save my friend from self-destruction. I was deeply angry when I drew this cartoon.

Cartoon 35. "Special Chow Down!"

Special chow was set up for the "sick," who to some appeared to be the healthiest among us. Since Cabanatuan was under U.S. officer control, the sick received slightly larger rations. In the camps in Japan, we were totally under Japanese military jurisdiction; the sick received reduced rations there.

Cartoon 36. "Sick Call"

When a POW did get sick or injured, the only aid available was charcoal. It took a lot to be sick enough to get some relief because nothing was available. You took what you could get and it was always less than you needed.

Cartoon 37. "Light Duty"

Even if the camp doctor gave permission for you to stay in camp because you were moderately sick and to not go out on a work detail, you were still assigned to "light duty" within the camp.

Cartoon 38. "'Zero Ward' Cabanatuan P.O.W. Camp No. 1"

The interior of the Zero Ward in Cabanatuan Hospital was horrible beyond description. I opened the door once to see for myself—this was the last place these guys were going to go. They were just skeletons sitting on crap cans or lying in their own excrement. Forty percent of the American POWs in Japanese camps (11,000 men) died of starvation and neglect or were killed outright; 2600 perished the first six months in Cabanatuan. Compare these figures with Europe, where approximately 1 percent, about 1100 American POWs, died in Nazi camps.

Cartoon 39. "Candy (?) Salesman"

Some of the more resourceful prisoners bartered for raw rice, sugar, and yeast. They ground the rice into flour by using a bottle on a hard surface and mixed the flour with sugar (very little as it was precious) and yeast to make something resembling candy or cake. This product was sold at a profit, and the cycle repeated. My buddy Eichmann and I were in this business for a while. We were separated when I was sent to Japan but located each other after the war. We stayed in close contact until his death in April 2011.

Cartoon 40. "Camp Cobbler"

Most of the time we were without shoes in Cabanatuan. The shoes we had before the surrender finally wore out in camp to the point of no repair. We resorted to making clogs out of 2x4 blocks with straps, which we called "go-aheads." Cobbler duty was very enviable.

Cartoon 41. "Barracks Barber"

Cigarettes were the main currency in camp, and guys would do odd jobs to get "paid." One of the men in the barracks would cut hair or give shaves for one or even two cigarettes, which was very expensive.

Cartoon 42. "A Prisoner's Prisoner"

The camp had its own brig to keep order. The guy in this cartoon had stolen some medicine from a fellow POW who died as a result. The thief was turned over to me, and I didn't treat him well. I refused to allow him to sit at the table during meals and wouldn't let him eat with utensils so he had to eat with his hands. I tried to make his life miserable but I didn't physically hurt him and nobody else did, either. I guess we all were just trying to survive ourselves and there was only so much we could do.

Cartoon 43. "Camp Guard"

We were placed in "shooting squads" of ten men. If one man escaped, the remaining squad members were shot. To prevent the execution of the innocent, a camp guard of American prisoners was established to prevent escape. We didn't feel bad about blowing the whistle on guys trying to escape.

Cartoon 44. "Butt Shootin'"

Many of the National Guard troops were quite undisciplined and, in my opinion, lacked the pride that the Marine Corps pounded into us. A Jap soldier would deliberately toss a cigarette butt on the ground and gloat as the poor creatures fought over it like hyenas at a kill.

Cartoon 45. "The News Center"

The head was the place where scuttlebutt (rumors) made the rounds.

Cartoon 46. "Bringing Home the Bacon"

A Navy chief petty officer was lucky enough to get the job of picking up supplies in a carabao cart.
Any job that would get you out of camp gave you the opportunity to obtain extra food and other goodies.

Cartoon 47. "Buying Chow or Throat Cutting Delux"

The few lucky prisoners who had work detail outside of the camps would sometimes have the opportunity to purchase eggs, sugar, or fruit from Filipino peddlers. Unfortunately, there were often a few who had enough money to bid up the prices to everyone's disadvantage. Profiteers were looked upon with contempt.

Cartoon 48. "Inflation"

In Cabanatuan, some POWs were lucky enough to get outside work details. This cartoon is a protest against profiteers. Many of the "affluent" camp-bound would bid up prices extremely high. A peso ("p") was very hard to obtain.

Cartoon 49. (left) "When Are Dem Cooks" (right) "'Quan' Shave"

(*left*) Much of the rice we received was dirty and full of sweepings. It usually contained weevils and other stuff from off the floor.

(*right*) Shaving was a problem in some camps. We were provided razor blades about twice a month. They were picked up and counted, and then reissued to us the next time. Prisoners attempted to sharpen the blades by oscillating them inside a glass. I shaved with my mess kit knife—it had not been confiscated—until somebody "borrowed" it to open up a can. But before my knife got borrowed, one day a Jap guard who was writing some orders broke the lead in his pencil. He saw my knife and gestured for it—I thought. "Damn, there goes my knife." Instead, he sharpened his pencil and presented my knife back to me, handle first. You just couldn't figure these Japs out!

Cartoon 50. "~~Irritating~~ Irrigating Project"

One of the jobs on the farm that utilized a great number of men was the water detail. Some of us attempted to spill as much water as possible on our way to the crops without being seen by a guard. Prisoners did not get much from the farm, mostly potato tops ("pipe stems")—the food grown on the farm was for the Japanese. We did try to smuggle something edible back into camp but the cost was a severe beating if we got caught. I hated working on the farms because there were too many guards.

Cartoon 51. "Hard Day's Pay or Come and Get Your Bun"

For a brief period at Cabanatuan we received a small, sweet, and very tasty bun for our labors on the farm. I would not even trade the bun for rice because that would contribute to the other guy's death.

Cartoon 52. "Cut in Pay or It Can't Last Forever (Not Even the Buns)"

Getting the buns for our farm labor didn't last forever—only for a few months.

Cartoon 53. Barracks Commissarys Arrive!!

About once a month we received a small amount of tea, sugar, cigarettes, etc., to be purchased with earnings from laboring on the farms. Two prisoners would generally have to combine their entire month's pay to afford a quarter pound of tea or a small container of curry powder.

Cartoon 54. "Wood Detail"

The wood detail was one of the better assignments we could get. It was my first detail, but it ended when the men who had been confined at O'Donnell arrived and I was assigned to the burial detail. Some of the Japanese seemed to respect us Marines. I even had one guard spell me at wood chopping. I held his rifle while he showed off for the work detail. And he later showed us how to field strip his rifle!

Cartoon 55. "Wood Detail Hard at Work"

Many of the Jap guards on the wood detail were kind to us when out of sight of their superiors. And many of the guards tried to learn English. We didn't get many opportunities to bathe so this creek was heaven—it was clear and the water was safe to drink.

Cartoon 56. "Woodsmen Retreat or Ants in Me Pants"

Wood cutting had its bad moments. The guards were not always sympathetic, either.

Cartoon 57. "House Wrecker Wrecks Wrong House"

One day I was out on a work detail where we were demolishing old barracks. I accidentally whacked a hornet's nest and suffered the consequences.

CAMP SAKURAJIMA, OSAKA, JAPAN

OCTOBER 1943 - MAY 1945

In September 1943 I was relocated from Camp Cabanatuan to Camp Sakurajima, near Osaka, after a voyage on the Taga Maru (nicknamed by the POWs as the Corral Maru), one of the "hell ships." It was frightening to be transferred; most POWs tried to avoid it. I don't know how the selection was made, but I believe some U.S. officers were involved in the decision. Unfortunately for them, however, most of the officers made their final trip on later hell ships. All the ships had been unmarked by the Japs and many were attacked and sunk by U.S. forces. (The hell ships are a story in themselves—at least as bad as the African slave ships because the Japs had no vested interest in keeping their prisoners alive.) While I was on the Taga, we were attacked by Allied submarines and even hit by a torpedo—thankfully a dud. The ship was sunk by a U.S. submarine only two months after we arrived in Japan.

In Sakurajima (the word means "cherry blossom") I was a slave laborer for the Osaka Iron Works. I worked as riveter, number 23 (number worn on my cap), on new ships being constructed down on the docks in the shipyard. Jap civilians, including women, also worked on these ships. The riveter position, because it was considered skilled labor, was the top position and as such it got respect. It was a relief to get out of camp away from the eyes of the guards.

Our Japanese work bosses (honchos) were totally in charge. After one of our B29 bombings of Osaka, I was assigned to a clean-up crew supervised by the Green Jackets (our civilian guards, a despicable lot). It was on this detail that I received one of my worst beatings. (Up till that point I had often been subjected to "slapsy-wapsy," a "fun game" which the Japanese subjected us prisoners too often. Two prisoners were forced to face one another and slap each other alternately on one side of the face and then the other. We learned how to pull our slaps but it happened enough to me that I believe some of the hearing loss in my left ear was caused by repeated blows during this game.)

Well, on this detail I was assigned the job of picking up debris and stacking it in a pile. Evidently I was not moving fast enough for a sad excuse of a Green Jacket named Taketa, for I heard him yell "Speedo!", a favorite term often used by the Japs to speed up the work. I gave him an insolent look since I, a riveter, was not used to taking orders from creeps like him (I had adapted to the Japanese caste system). Taketa-san picked up a 2x2 post a little longer than a baseball bat and screamed, "Kiotski!" (attention!). I dropped my load and snapped to the stiff Japanese-style attention, and he proceeded to clobber me about the head and shoulders, swinging the board like a baseball bat. I remember only the first three blows.

A lot of time went by before I regained consciousness, so much so that the blood in my hair and on my jacket was dry. I was pulling debris from one of the buildings and turned to the worker next to me and asked what happened. Did I fall down? When did he stop working me over? Why did he stop? When my friend realized I was serious, he told me that I had not fallen, although they couldn't believe it possible. Taketa had been in a frenzy and pounded on me until he was tired. He finally stopped and I had evidently about-faced and went back to work. I still don't remember going to work, lunch, or anything until the instant I came to with a splitting headache that obscured the rest of my pain. I probably hadn't fallen down during or after the beating because we had been conditioned to avoid showing fear or falling to the ground when being beaten to avoid antagonizing the Japanese, who considered it a form of weakness (part of their "unique culture" they were defending against Western imperialism). My survival can probably be attributed to early training in boxing in high school. I had evidently instinctively rolled with the blows. Also, I had vowed never to let the little bastards kill me.

My riveter honcho was a Jap called Kono, and we actually got along rather well—at lunchtime we would even eat together. He didn't have to do anything but supervise, though he did on occasion spell me when I got tired of riveting. He wasn't crazy about the war either. Kono trusted me, and because I could write his name in Japanese, I had some freedom at work to move around. I would get the rivets and equipment when I went to the supply outfit and sign his name. There was an understanding between us to such an extent that one day, when the scaffolding above me came loose and hit me in the head and knocked me out, I came to with my head on his lap and a wet rag on my forehead.

There was this one Jap civilian—a guy who worked on scaffolding above me—who would deliberately try to burn me and drop heavy things on me. He might well have been responsible for the scaffolding collapsing on me. Well, one day when I was riveting I tossed some of the hot rivets onto his clothing. His clothing ignited and he fell off the scaffolding and died. Lucky for me the Jap honchos thought he had accidently fallen and didn't know he was on fire.

I "borrowed" (stole) my forge from a Jap civilian crew and painted a white star on the side of it. Of course I stole the paint. It was common to try to sabotage whenever you could. I would drop equipment and rivets "by accident" into the water or down cracks. The rivets would get really hot and I burned down a scaffold one day by leaving a pile of hot rivets on the wooden platform at lunchtime—I had left my air hose where it gently blew air on the pile of rivets. When we would finish building a ship the Japs would actually invite us to watch the launch and celebration! I did this "job" for about a year and a half until the Allied fire bombings destroyed the docks in May 1945.

PART 3. CAMP SAKURAJIMA, JAPAN, CARTOONS

Cartoon 58 (sketch). "Sakurajima POW Camp, Osaka, Japan"

This sketch is drawn from memory on arrival at the Akenobe POW camp.

Cartoon 59. "Why Wasn't I Captured by the Germans?!"

On arrival we found the accomodations left something to be desired, especially for the tallest among us.

Cartoon 60. "Sketch of Fireplace"

The fireplace, prime real estate, was just a pile of charcoal pieces, no vent, at the end of the barracks. Each barracks received a small ration of charcoal, about four handfuls, for warmth in the winter—an impossible effort, as the barracks had no insulation or even caulking. The charcoal did provide a minute source of heat for those who saved their meager rations or scrounged tidbits for later.

Cartoon 61. "Watch Your Helethh"

The interpreter at Sakurajima, a most hated individual, constantly warned us to watch our "heleth." We were forced to arise before dawn in the sleet and snow for taiso (exercise), which consisted of running two laps around the compound followed by scrubbing ourselves down with the stiff brushes that we also used for cleaning our dishes. The outdoor wooden racks for our morning ablutions as well as for washing our clothes were often frozen over.

Cartoon 62. "Steady Cock This Won't Hurt—Much! or An Open Arm Welcome (Wide Open!)

Our sick bay had very little medicine, but we were lucky enough to have a rather sadistic British corpsman.

Cartoon 63. "A Sentry's Sentry! or Pretty Good Picking"

As in Cabanatuan, we had prisoners who stood watch and kept a log of those leaving the barracks to go to the benjo (toilet). The cold weather exacerbated our bladder problems. Sometimes the Jap guard would join the POW sentry. Contrary to the cleanliness stereotype, many of the Japs had lice.

Cartoon 64. "Klim Kan Klub"

Awakening ten to twenty times a winter's night drove some individuals to rather desperate measures. Many of the Red Cross boxes we received contained a powdered milk product called "Klim" ("milk" spelled backwards), a very relished item. These cans were valuable for a variety of reasons, including for use as chamber pots. However, prisoners who resorted to this device were ostracized because they would frequently spill some of the contents on the boys below or nearby. Good hygiene was essential for survival and we despised these guys. One time I punched somebody out for spilling the contents of his can on me.

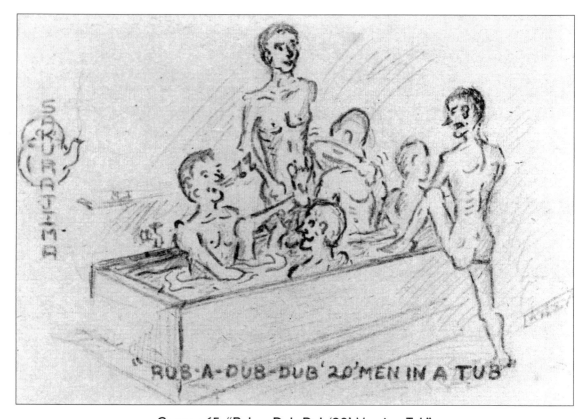

Cartoon 65. "Rub-a-Dub-Dub '20' Men in a Tub"

The camp was made up of about 200 British troops and 100 Americans. Hot water for all was provided on our "rest day" twice a month. But a large number of the British complement and a few Americans were loathe to take advantage of this accomodation. So all POWs were marched to the bath house at bayonet point and forced into the bath. All well and good, except the British hut went first. Though the procedure was to wash down and rinse with a small bucket before entering the Japanese-style community tub (capacity about 20), the prisoners were so dirty and so hurried by the guards that the water was soup by the time our barracks was summoned. Those of us who bathed every day with cold water couldn't wait to wash off with cold water after our "hot bath."

Cartoon 66. "Strafin' or Caught wid da Goods!"

"Strafing" was the routine shakedown for forbidden items. Prisoners would be beaten for possession of knives, razors, pens, pencils, blank paper, etc. One time in our barracks we had a flash inspection. I was seated at a table slicing up a bun with my knife and looked to see a Jap at the door. I continued cutting and eating the small pieces, trying to carry on but thinking to myself, "Oh shit!" The Jap just passed me by.

Cartoon 67. "Tsh! Tsh! These Faulty Paddles! or What! This Ain't My Bowl?!"

Of course, this never really did happen to me, Ni Jm San Bon (No. 23). I survived. We would put our numbers on our bowls and turn them so the server could not see whose bowl it was.

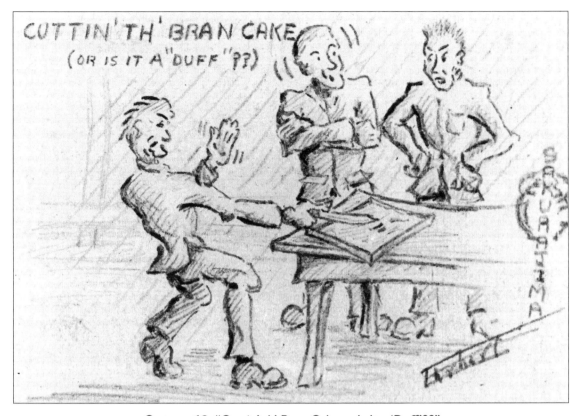

Cartoon 68. "Cuttin' th' Bran Cake or Is It a 'Duff'??"

Occasionally, the cooks would obtain a supply of rice bran, which they made into a rather bland, sugarless cake (quite a delicacy for us). The division and rationing were always carefully observed.

Cartoon 69. "Ain't They on Rations?"

In general, the cooks fared better than the workers and always had fat guts. A few worked for the Japanese, often to great advantage. This fellow is feeding a rabbit, exclusively for Japanese consumption. And often the rabbits' rations were more than OUR rations!

Cartoon 70. "Taken by Mistake (?)"

Not all prisoners were honorable.

Cartoon 71. "The Weight Is There or 'Nuts' in Lieu of Rice (also Bolts)

The response to almost any complaint regarding rations was "the weight's there." Of course, that weight included debris in the rice. This cartoon is slightly exaggerated.

Cartoon 72. "The Weight's There or A Bun Now for One Tomorrow"

Due to size variation, the weight issue was especially true in regard to the buns. Often, because we were literally starving, a stronger willed POW would trade a weaker willed person a small bun he had received for a bun the next day, knowing that the odds were favorable that he would get a larger one the next day.

Cartoon 73. "The Weight Is There (?)"

Another cartoon about this life-or-death matter. In most cases, the weight was not necessarily always there—thus our vigilance!

Cartoon 74. "The Weight's Not There!!"

Most of the POWs weighed about a hundred pounds. The sick weighed less and were usually given reduced rations since if you didn't "work for the Emperor," you didn't eat.

Cartoon 75. "Two Weeks' 'Veg' Ration (The Turnips Arrive!!)"

Two weeks' ration for all of us—mostly daikons—except for the rice, arrived on a three-wheeled motorcycle.

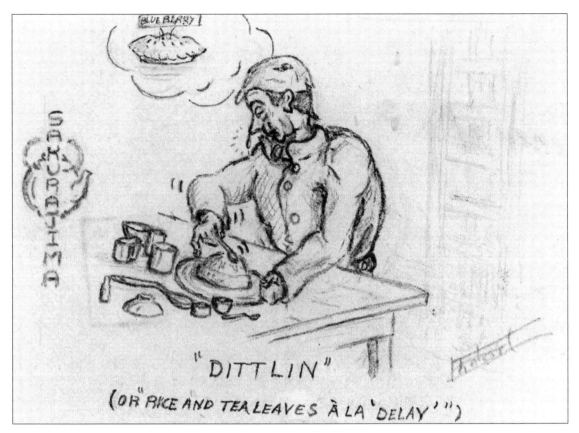

Cartoon 76. "Dittlin or Rice and Tea Leaves a la 'Delay'"

A few prisoners "played around" with their food and concocted imaginary dishes such as pie. They often mixed rice with tea leaves for bulk, extending the meal for as long as possible and frequently licking the bowl when finished.

Cartoon 77. "Standing Room Only or Save Some Seats for the Sick"

After a meager breakfast of rice and thin soup (often only water and soy sauce), we were marched to a streetcar stop to go to work on the docks. On occasion we had a few civilians on board the streetcars, and their rush for seats was chaotic. Many of the more disciplined of us frowned on this practice. However, this method of boarding was typical of the Japs.

Cartoon 78. "Smoke Gets in Your Eyes or Even the Fireman Has His Troubles"

The prisoners at this camp worked at the Osaka Iron Works building oil tankers and corvettes. As seen in this cartoon, one of our jobs during the internment at Sakurajima was fireman for a rivet crew. I practiced very hard tossing rivets during our training period. Firing rivets turned out to have a few negatives, however. In the sleet and snow you froze in the back and cooked in the front, while hot coals popped into your eyes. There were times when a Jap welder would try to blind you with a flash from his electrodes or spatter you with slag. Once a civilian worker "accidentally" dropped a sledgehammer from about fifty feet above me, missing me by inches. Another time a large steel plate fell from above, barely missing me. The Jap workers seemed to like going after me, perhaps because I was a stationary target.

Cartoon 79. "Did I Do Something Wrong?"

For lunch the rivet crews were rewarded with an extra bowl of thick rice soup containing a few vegetables for driving a minimum of three hundred rivets the previous day. However, the Japs insisted we put the rice bowls in a certain order,and sometimes guys would reach in the middle of the table to grab a bowl that had more food than the others. If caught, you'd get "whacked."

Cartoon 80. "Gash!"

We all wanted to be on the best crews because they would be assigned the plates on the hulls of the ships. These open, flat spaces allowed us to reach the three hundred rivet quota, rewarding us with the extra noon meal. We tried to avoid being assigned to the tight spots and difficult corners because we could drive fewer rivets at these locations. Periodically, the Japs would increase the requirement to 325 or 360 rivets a day , but for some reason productivity would decrease significantly, sometimes averaging in the low two hundreds. The Japs would then return the quota to three hundred, and the up and down quota cycle would start again.

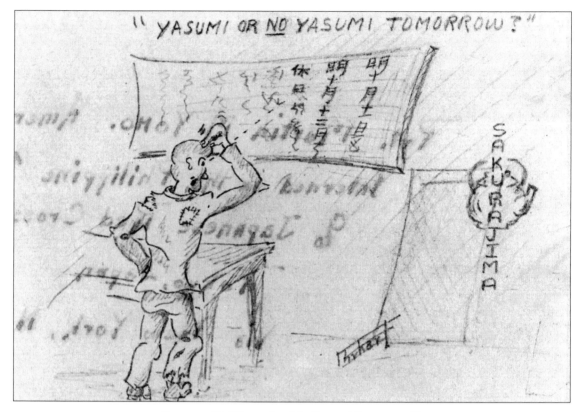

Cartoon 81. "Yasumi or No Yasumi Tomorrow?"

Our "work week" was fifteen days long. On our one day of rest (yasumi) we were required to perform Japanese close order drill all morning. We were a military camp and even wore cast-off Japanese army uniforms. Our only distinction from the Japanese (besides our physical characteristics) was a red strip on our caps. The afternoons were spent policing the barracks and cleaning our clothes, after which we could read the few books and ancient Reader's Digests the Japs would issue for the day. Often we were serenaded with Japanese music and once in a great while even a western tune.

Cartoon 82. "A Work Hater"

Some tried to make the sick list the hard way. It was not uncommon for POWs to deliberately hurt themselves, even by breaking arms or legs, to avoid work details.

Cartoon 83. "Tomorrow's Yasumi or One More Bridge to Cross"

Camp Sakurajima was located on an island in a river. After a long day's work, we knew we were almost "home" when we reached the bridge. All that remained was roll call (tinko), sometimes a lecture or assembly to witness an unlucky prisoner's punishment, and finally chow and sleep, interrupted by frequent trips to the latrine.

Cartoon 84. "One Between Three or Individual (?) Red Cross Boxes Are Issued"

As an inducement for us to work harder, most of our mail was withheld for special occasions. Any Red Cross boxes or parcels from home were usually released at Christmas. Often the Red Cross packages had to be divided between two or three men. In the three and a half years of confinement, I received an average of about one and a half parcels per year (one English Red Cross, one personal, and the rest American Red Cross). I received five or six letters a year. "We give you mail" and "Watch your heleth" were the Japanese interpreters' most understandable English phrases.

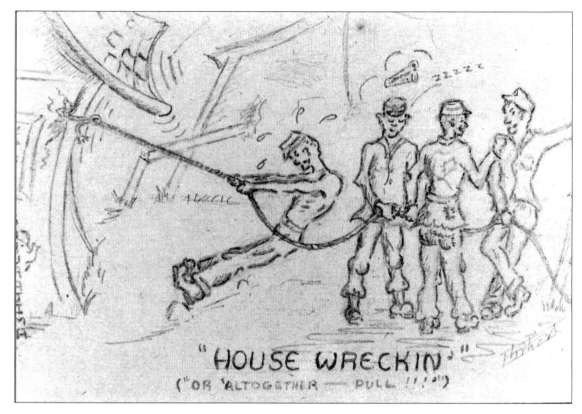

Cartoon 85. "House Wreckin' or Altogether—Pull!!!"

The fire bombing of Osaka by the Americans was one of our most delightful, though frightening, experiences. The entire city was destroyed. The bombing ended our work in the shipyard so our new job consisted of tearing down many of the remaining flammable wooden structures.

CAMP AKENOBE, JAPAN

MAY – SEPTEMBER 1945

After the fire-bombing of Osaka (the shipyards having been targets for our bombers), the Japs moved us to a different camp about seventy-five miles inland to the northwest, Akenobe No. 6B. Akenobe was a mining camp in a rather beautiful mountain setting. My first work detail at this camp was helping build a rope bridge across a small creek, leading up to the mine entrance. The honcho on this detail was a sympathetic Korean guy about my age and we got along really well. He warned me to try to avoid working in the mines and did what he could to delay my transfer to that duty. But time ran out—the bridge was finally built and I was assigned to work in the Mitsubishi copper mine.

The reason I was warned not to work in the mine was because of the miserable conditions in the mine and because of the mine's Jap honcho, nicknamed The Madman. He was notorious for screaming and hitting the POWs, and he was reputed to have driven one Brit insane. I was assigned to The Madman as a stope driller, and things got really interesting the first few days. Stope drilling required the use of a seventy-five-pound drill (I weighed only one hundred pounds at the time) with bits anywhere from twelve inches to several feet long. It was very hard and dangerous work.

The Madman trained me to use the stope drill. Every time I made a mistake, he jumped up and down, screaming and hitting me. And every time he behaved like that, I would turn off the equipment and sit down. He would continue to scream and hit. I would then use hand signals to say that he should be quiet, to wait a minute and slow down. I tried to convey to him that I wanted to get out of the mine as much as he did, that I was a good worker, and that he needed to leave me alone. Finally he would leave me, coming back later to see that I was making progress. Eventually he even quit referring to me as "omae," a lower expression for "you," and began using "anata," a form that was more respectful and formal.

To reach our stope, The Madman and I had to walk about a quarter-mile along the first drift, and then climb five or six levels on rickety wooden ladders. I would follow my honcho and carry the explosives in a large wooden box strapped on my back like a backpack. To my amazement, a Jap lugged the heavy steel rock drills up and down the ladders for our use. I did my best to break and "round-off" as much equipment as possible, so the poor guy had to return often with new replacements. My sabotage served two purposes: It destroyed valuable equipment and made the Jap work harder. Since the Japs were treating me as slave labor while starving me to death, it seemed like a good thing.

I had to "blow" a certain amount of ore each day. I would meet my quota before noon, then after lunch I would take off and look for watercress, snakes, and anything I might be able to quan back in camp. It was during these afternoon breaks that I would also draw some of my cartoons.

PART 4. CAMP AKENOBE, JAPAN, CARTOONS

Cartoon 86 (sketch). "Camp Akenobe No. 6B"

Akenobe was a mining camp in a beautiful mountain setting.

Cartoon 87 (sketch). "Mitsubishi Mine Entrance"

For the first month in this camp my work detail was building a bridge across a small creek. My boss was a very sympathetic Korean about my age. He was a good man, and I'd be happy to have him for a friend today.

Cartoon 88. "Lower Bay Laments"

As in Camp Sakurajima, we were quartered in drafty, uninsulated, wood buildings. We slept on bamboo decks stacked three high, with just enough space between to allow us to sit up. The men on the lower decks had some special problems, given their location.

Cartoon 89. "Flea's Bother Ya Much Last Nite"

Akenobe had a plague of fleas. One evening I was taking my blanket from the clothesline where I'd left it to sun during the day. I felt an itching and crawling on my legs. I lifted my pant leg to find that my ankle and lower calf were absolutely black with fleas.

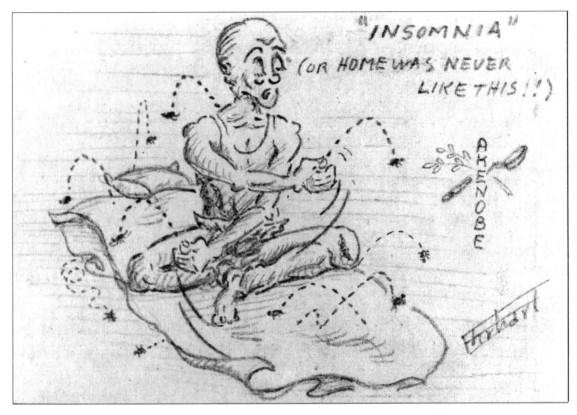

Cartoon 90. "Insomnia or Home Was Never Like This!!"

Sleep was impossible. I rigged a hammock out of my shelterhalf and strung it between two posts in my bay. This offered some relief from the vermin.

Cartoon 91. "Quick Change Artists or 'cuze My Rush!"

At Akenobe as elsewhere when we went to relieve ourselves we expected blood and mucous in our stools. Everyone had dysentery—always a major killer and a constant threat. The symptoms would stop, only to appear a month or so later, and we never knew if the next episode would be the fatal one.

Cartoon 92. "Pessimist Delux"

By this time at Akenobe, even the optimists were cropping their hair for hygiene.

Cartoon 93. "One Between Six!"

There were very few clothing issues, and when there were, the items had to be somehow divided between several POWs. Here it was socks. I don't remember having socks to wear, and throughout most of the early days we seldom had shoes. How do you divide one pair of socks between six prisoners? (We didn't have any scissors.)

Cartoon 94. "Camp Amusements or The Needlework Guild"

I don't remember anyone sewing for fun. But sewing and darning were necessary parts of prison life.

Cartoon 95. "Lobbin' It Out"

In both Sakurajima and Akenobe, I was the mess cook for my squad. It was my job to pick up the buckets of rice and soup, portion them out, and return the buckets to the galley. Filling the rice bowls required great effort, as the server was under everybody's intense scrutiny to be sure no one would get an extra grain of rice. Why I was chosen for this task is not known. Perhaps it was trust or maybe they feared me or maybe they were afraid someone worse would take over.

Cartoon 96. "The Doorway (?)"

After I had been mess cook for a couple of years, I started to realize that I was the only one stupid enough to have accepted the job. POWs— typical of most soldiers and sailors—congregated around the doorways, much to the dismay of the duty personnel. It was tough to manuever through the guys and keep the chow in the buckets at the same time.

Cartoon 97. "Gumy Rice"

Rice was our staple, though not always prepared to our liking. But regardless of how it was cooked, we always eagerly looked forward to the the next meal the moment that the last grain of the current meal was eaten.

Cartoon 98. "Lunch?!! or We Give You Bread!"

The Brits were always complaining that bread was "the staff of life." They got their wish when a small bun was substituted for our bowl of rice for the midday "meal." This substitution was not appreciated by most of the U.S. troops since we didn't believe it was nearly as nutritious as rice, or as filling. But it was delicious. At Akenobe I kept up the practice of never trading cigarettes for another man's food, or knowingly doing anything else to endanger another POW. I did on several occasions accept the offer of an Englishman's evening rice for my noon bun.

Cartoon 99. "Home from Work or Rations on the Q.T."

We were especially starved for vitamins and protein. Consequently, on the way to the mine, or when out of the mine in the case of the drillers, we would search for anything that might possibly be edible. Getting caught trying to smuggle anything into camp could result in a beating.

Cartoon 100. "Tea or Tobacco or Just Leaves??"

Of course, most of us risked getting kicked around a little to bring our hoards back to camp. Then came the problem of deciding what was what since often we jammed anything we thought was edible in our pockets or in secret compartments.

Cartoon 101. "Green Pastures or Chow Down!!"

Grazing was the prudent thing to do, although sometimes a POW would choose the wrong plant and suffer the consequences. Occasionally I was lucky to find watercress, but anything to fill the void in my belly helped, even mulberry leaves.

Cartoon 102. "Tug-o-War or A Snake Looses His Tail"

One day I was one of the rare individuals fortunate enough to catch a snake. I was allowed to cook it on a corner of the fire. It was wonderful but bland—it would have been nice to have had salt. I could never understand why something as abundant as salt would be so precious. It was extremely difficult to obtain salt in the camps and very little was ever provided to us. I had a very small tin box that I kept salt in. That tin box was one of my most precious belongings.

Cartoon 103. "The Mystery of Missin' Lunch Box"

We always brought a ration of rice to work, and sometimes we either hung it outside or if we were near hot equipment placed it close by to stay warm. But if your lunch was out of your sight, there was the possibility it might get stolen. Thieves were despised, but I believe our theft rate was extremely low considering the extent of our deprivation.

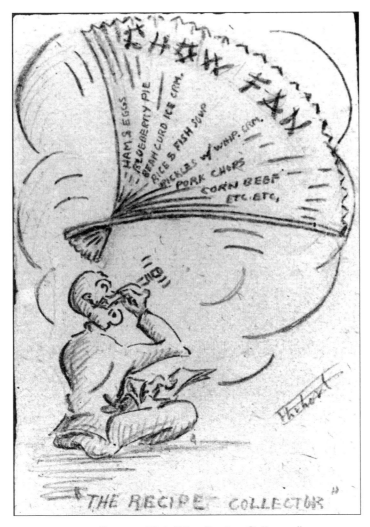

Cartoon 104. "The Recipe Collector"

Our obsession with food never ceased. Hunger was so great that all other thoughts were totally eclipsed. Almost every POW made copious lists of recipes, many outrageous. The only mention of the opposite sex was at Christmas time. A month or so before Christmas the cooks would hold back a small portion of the food ration to build up a supply to give us enough to fill our shrunken stomachs for one day. We made makeshift ornaments for decorating anything resembling a Christmas tree, and then our conversation would drift to home, wives, and girls.

Cartoon 105. "A Cook There Was or Back to Duty"

Sometimes a cook would be sent back to outside duty. In this cartoon he is the fat one.

Cartoon 106. "Carbide Lamps Are Issued!!"

All those who worked in the mine were taught first to use carbide lamps. Some POWs had a great deal of trouble learning to adjust them and they'd flare up. Once, when I was working in my stope, my light blew out after somebody blasted down the drift. I sat alone in the dark for what seemed like hours until finally my honcho came back. The dark was indescribable. The black pressed in on you like you were under water.

Cartoon 107. "Come on Yanks! or One More Hole 'till Chow"

During the first week or so on the job, a British POW worked near the face of the stope while I worked the rear. This guy was a whiner and a klutz—he kept The Madman screaming. The unlucky Brit took some of The Madman's pressure off me, but I was glad when he finally convinced the medics that he was too sick to work.

Cartoon 108. "Typical Driller Busy Drilling (?)"

Getting the bit stuck up in the rock happened way too frequently.

Cartoon 109. "Oh! To Be an Octupus!"

Getting impaled by the bit never happened to us at Akenobe as far as I know. But it was certainly possible since it took three hands to operate the equipment.

Cartoon 110. "Yasumi Day (?)"

Just as in Camp Sakurajima, we got a yasumi day (day off) every fifteen days. But of course we still had to do chores such as washing our clothes, collecting wood, and cleaning the barracks.

LIBERATION

AUGUST 1945

Sometime in the middle of August 1945, the wail of the air raid sirens no longer punctuated our days. We sensed something had happened. The Japanese commandant asked our commanding officer what time we would like reveille in the morning but emphasized that the Japanese calls would still be sounded.

Later, after it had become clear that the war was over and after the Japs had left camp, a British trooper ripped open a pillow he had carried with him for over three and a half years and produced a Union Jack. Not to be outdone, we Americans scrounged any materials that were red, white, or blue and by working all night finally produced a very pitiful but very proud American flag.

At 8 am the following day, all of us—British and American— stood in formation and ran colors. I am sure I was not alone, but at the sound of "To the Colors" I choked up. I could hardly breathe, and, try as I might, I couldn't stop my eyes from filling and flowing over. This experience and that of the surrender at Corregidor are burned into my soul forever.

Our officers took charge, reorganized the camp, and issued new camp orders. I, as one of the U.S. Marines, was assigned to military police duty outside the camp. We wore a makeshift MP band on our arm and were to secure order outside the camp. Surprisingly, there was very little retribution. Both U.S. and British troops, in my opinion, were determined not to lower · themselves to the level of the Bushido culture (which refers to the Samurai behavior). There were a couple of lapses, but they were minor.

Repatriation was a slow process. Like all of the former prisoners in Japan, we were first sprayed with DDT and issued fresh clothing and toiletries. A lot of the guys were then sent to the Philippines to fatten them up before going home. Others like me were flown to Guam, where

I was detained for about a month before getting a transport home. Although prisoners were said to have priority just behind the mail, the Red Cross did arrange a phone call to my parents so they knew I was alive and okay.

I arrived in San Diego rather late—the welcome home signs were gone but the wonderful Red Cross ladies welcomed us with small bags of toothpaste, razors, and other toiletries. I was finally transported to Oak Knoll Naval Hospital in Oakland, California, and discharged at Treasure Island in San Francisco on April 29, 1946.

It was stateside where I first learned about the WACs, WAVEs, BAMs, and the many changes of the last three and a half years. It is also where I learned about the A-bomb. The atomic bomb was our savior beyond all doubt. There was no way we POWs could have survived the winter in that mountain camp. Americans today haven't the slightest understanding of the Japanese Bushido Code held sacred by not only the military but the majority of the general populace. They were ready to fight to the death—every man, woman, and child. Also, it was well known that all of the POWs would have been killed rather than left alive to reveal the anguish they endured. The toll in human lives would have been devastating had there been an Allied landing on the islands.

One last thing. Cartoon 111 marks one of the heroic efforts of the war not adequately recognized. Our camp was nestled among several mountains. Shortly after the end of hostilities, a C54 (B29 cargo airplane) circled our camp, which we had marked with large letters on the rooftops as "POW." The pilot of the huge aircraft dove between the mountaintops and unloaded his treasure of canned meat, soup, chocolate, fruit, cigarettes, and other goodies we had not seen in nearly four years. Most of the supplies floated gently down on parachutes, but a very significant number came catapulting down like projectiles, some severing utility poles and causing us to dive for cover. There were no injuries. Here is one Marine who has nothing but admiration (though I hate to admit it!), for that "Fly-Fly-Boy" who piloted his monstrous aircraft into that hole and pulled up, barely missing the mountains on the other side, and then returned to repeat the display. Thank you!

PART 5. LIBERATION CARTOONS

Cartoon 111. "The Best Bombing Yet !! 30 Aug '45"

We knew the war was over when we were not ordered to work. Soon our B29s started dropping supplies into our camp.

Cartoon 112. "Pennies from Heaven (via B-Ni-Ju Ku)"

Many former POWS gorged themselves, some becoming violently ill. I was happy to know that I would live to lead a normal life again, and carefully, though with extreme difficulty, limited myself to mostly rice. I stuffed myself with rice while carefully supplementing it slowly with richer nourishment dropped from the heavens. I wasn't taking any more chances!

Cartoon 113. "Yank Meets Yank"

Our officers commandeered, or somehow obtained, a train to take us to Yokohama. The U.S. prisoners marched out of camp with our little flag flying in front of the column to the waiting boxcars. We were met by an airborne unit that wore strange uniforms with helmets similar to those of the Germen soldiers at the beginning of the war. Our helmets and most of our equipment were of World War I vintage.

Cartoon 114. "All That Then a Navy Transport Too!!!"

When they discovered I was still there, I was placed aboard the next transport. I believe it was a Liberty Ship, perhaps one that my dad worked on while I was building tankers for Japan as my slave labor job. There were so many of us that I was billeted topside, where often we were in the way of the ship's crew during their cleaning duty.

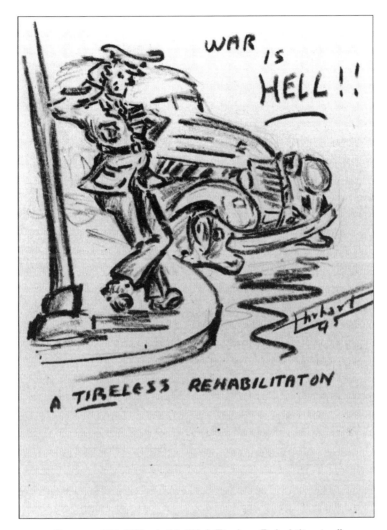

Cartoon 115. "War Is Hell!! A Tireless Rehabilitation"

Rubber rationing was still in effect when I returned to the States. Many cars had tires so worn they could not stay inflated. When I finally arrived in Oakland, my hometown seemed strange after five-and-a-half years. I got off the bus and looked around, trying to orient myself. I gave up and called a cab. The driver was nice and very interested in my story. He stayed at the curb until he saw my folks greet me. They weren't expecting me as yet. My mother opened the door. All I said was "Hi, Mom, I'm home."

Biographical Sketches

ROBERT EHRHART is a retired engineer for the Department of Water Resources in Sacramento, California. He served in the 4th Marines in World War II and became a prisoner of war following the surrender of the Philippines in May 1942. Bob, born in 1923 in Oakland, California, had joined the Marine reserves in 1940 at the age of 17 and was called to active duty while still a senior in high school. After basic training he was stationed in the Philippines at the Cavite Naval Yard and assigned to an anti-aircraft unit. His unit was later transferred to Bataan, then Corregidor and Fort Hughes on Caballo Island. Following the U.S. surrender, Bob's three-and-a-half years as a POW of imperial Japan began. He was assigned to Camp Cabanatuan on Luzon then relocated to two POW camps in Japan, Sakurajima and Akenobe, surviving a hell ship and slave labor. After the surrender of Japan in 1945, Bob recovered in military hospitals and was honorably discharged in 1946. He was accepted at the University of California, Berkeley, and graduated in 1950 with a BS in mechanical engineering. Bob settled in Carmichael, California, with his wife, Winnie, after their wedding in 1957. They had a long and happy life together until her death in 2001. Bob is still active, enjoying his hobbies of photography and world travel.

JAN THOMPSON is a professor in the department of Radio, Television and Digital Media at Southern Illinois University, Carbondale. She serves as president of the nonprofit educational organization, The American Defenders of Bataan & Corregidor Memorial Society. A documentary filmmaker, Jan has produced several works based on the prisoner-of-war experience. Her feature-length film, *Never the Same: The Prisoner of War Experience*, is narrated by Loretta Swit and features the voices of Ed Asner, Alec Baldwin, Jamie Farr, Mike Farrell, Robert Forster, Christopher Franciosa, Robert Loggia, Christopher Murray, Don Murray, John O'Hurley, Kathleen Turner, Robert Wagner, and Sam Waterston. These distinguished actors came together to dramatize the diaries, poems, drawings, and cartoons of POWs. Jan's earlier film, *The Tragedy of Bataan*, is a half-hour documentary with a five-part radio series narrated by Alec Baldwin. Several of Bob Ehrhart's cartoons are featured in both *Never the Same* and *The Tragedy of Bataan*.

20516508R00090

Made in the USA
San Bernardino, CA
13 April 2015